P9-DHM-346

PostSecret

Confessions on Life, Death, and God

8561

PostSecret
13345 Copper Ridge Rd.
Germantown, Maryland
20874

Also by **Frank Warren**

PostSecret

My Secret

The Secret Lives of Men and Women

A Lifetime of Secrets

PostSecret: Confessions

WILLIAM MORROW *An Imprint of* HarperCollins*Publishers*

on Life, Death, and God

Frank Warren

HarperCollins books may be purchased for educational, business, or sales promotional use. For information please write: Special Markets Department, HarperCollins Publishers, 10 East 53rd Street, New York, NY 10022.

Designed by Joy O'Meara

Library of Congress Cataloging-in-Publication Data

Warren, Frank (Frank C.), 1964–
    Postsecret : confessions on life, death, and God / Frank Warren. — 1st ed.
        p.   cm.
ISBN 978-0-06-185933-5
1. Self-disclosure—Miscellanea. 2. Postcards. I. Title. II. Title: Postsecret.
BF697.5.S427W374 2009
741.6'83—dc22

2009025378

---

11   12   13   lp/wz   10   9   8   7   6   5   4

Acknowledgments

I would like to offer a personal thank-you to my friends listed below who made this book possible, and a special note of appreciation to Kathy, who has faithfully delivered hundreds of thousands of postcards to my mailbox with kindness and care, as if the secrets were sacred.

Brian DeFiore, Rebecca Hoffberger, Reese Butler, Cassie Jones, Lynn Grady, Brianne Halverson, Shawn Nicholls, Paul Fireman, Kelley Stillwell, Nicole Keimer, Brian Cotlove, Sebastian Schultheiss, Sarah Amspaugh, Hilary Leister, Paige Morency-Brassard, Erin Kowalski, P.S.C., T.C., and F.F.

In memory of Kristin Brooks, Chris Dittman, Robbie Coleman, Dave Cunha, Dennis Harrod, and Cindy.

As always, I wish to thank each individual artist whose confession, whether reproduced in these pages or not, helps reveal our hidden unity.

Foreword

I was banging on the door, then I realized I was knocking from inside.

—Rumi

The very first PostSecret postcard I can remember reading was: "I am a Southern Baptist Pastor's Wife. No one knows that I do not believe in God." Its exasperated, pure, in-your-face rawness inspired me to ask PostSecret's creator, my friend Frank Warren, if he had received any other high-octane, big-subject secrets about life, death, religion, faith, and God. Out from his sky-high stacks, Frank deftly pulled dozens of secrets—among them a polar opposite to the faith secret provided by the pastor's wife. It read: "I am an editor for a large online atheist newsletter and I believe in GOD!!!"

Frank was sitting on a gold mine of full-frontal truthful expressions of belief—incredibly revealing and engaging, and capable of providing a real insight into what we human beings actually believe. I asked Frank if he could possibly take the time to curate a PostSecret mini-exhibition that could run as a powerful visual undercurrent to the many works of art produced by my self-taught artists. I was already curating these works for our eleventh mega-show, "All Faiths Beautiful: From Atheism to Zoroastrianism, Respect for Diversity of Belief," which ran in 2007 and 2008 at the American Visionary Art Museum in Baltimore.

The exhibition started with Frank's own faith secret (see the epilogue) and grew to include more than three hundred other PostSecret revelations about belief—some tragic, others playful, even hilarious. These secrets set the table for a raw and utterly honest feast on what doubts and convictions lie hidden among us all: From the Orthodox rabbi who so loved the beauty of Christmas in New York to those who simply used their 4-by-6-inch card to address God directly, either in thankfulness or to plead for His account in the loss of their child.

Frank's collaboration with our museum has been a mutually rich partnership right from the start. Our nationally known museum is devoted to intuitive artistry, and Frank credits it with helping to inspire his own work with PostSecret. In turn, Frank has taught us what truly pleases a crowd. Since the museum opened on Thanksgiving 1995, we have enjoyed many fruitful collaborations with a range of celebrities and true visionaries. Yet only with Frank and his PostSecret exhibit have we ever had to stay open for hours past our usual closing time. Frank's gentle, always respectful way of sharing truths—those that delight us and those that cause us to weep—caused long, patient lines to form all around our museum whenever he would come for an event.

The entire PostSecret experiment is a love song freeing one unique voice after another. To all of those individuals who got up the courage to reveal their authentic selves in a PostSecret card, I thank you for giving all of us a chance to deepen our own truths. That your voices have now found their way into a book gives testament to their enduring importance.

Openly and truthfully,
Rebecca Alban Hoffberger
Founder and Director, American Visionary Art Museum

Introduction

When I started collecting secrets in 2004, it felt like a creative prank. I invited strangers to artistically share their deepest secret on a postcard and mail it to me, anonymously. In four years, I have carefully pulled nearly a half-million postcards from my mailbox, and over a quarter-billion people have visited www.postsecret.com.

The secrets come from all continents, in many languages, uncovering our rich inner diversity while reminding us of our deeper unity. I have tried to bring these silent voices together to narrate our stories in five PostSecret books, in PostSecret events held around the country, and in various art exhibitions.

This book, *PostSecret: Confessions on Life, Death, and God*, was inspired by a collection of more than three hundred postcards that were part of an exhibit at the American Visionary Art Museum called "All Faiths Beautiful." The never-before-seen secrets between these pages were chosen to expose the common landscape of our private lives—from our embarrassing desires to our hidden acts of kindness; from the private prayers of atheists to the voiceless doubt of believers.

In addition to the postcards, I've included three short stories that show how finding the courage to share secrets can bring meaning, empathy, and special people into our lives.

The PostSecret Project no longer feels like a prank to me. I still get secrets that make me laugh, but I also receive postcards that have been transformative. I've witnessed how the project has changed people's lives, including my own.

I've seen secrets bring to life a hidden world that can inspire and comfort.

I've seen how the very act of sharing a secret can make it true.

I've seen how thousands of secrets, like different verses to the same song, sing of the search for that one special person we can tell all our secrets to.

I have seen how a collection of earnest secrets can challenge each of us to liberate our own.

I believe that every PostSecret book tells a story about us. I do not know what kind of story this book will be for you. For me it feels like a mystery—one that ends without resolution but leaves us with a greater sense of awe and wonder about our secrets, our relationships, and ourselves.

CAL 2309
California Dreaming.
Is it ok to be a scientist but still have faith?
Post Secret
13345 Copper Ridge Rd
Germantown, MD
20874
Navajo Jewelry
USA 2c
by California Scene®
(858)635-9400
www.calscene.com

I FOUND THIS INSIDE A
MAGAZINE ON AN AIRPLANE.
AS SOON AS I ARRIVED HOME,
I TOOK THE RING I'VE HAD
IN MY POCKET FOR TWO YEARS OUT
AND PROPOSED TO MY GIRLFRIEND
IN THE MIDDLE OF THE AIRPORT.

SHE SAID YES.

This is your
moment.
The right time
is NOW!

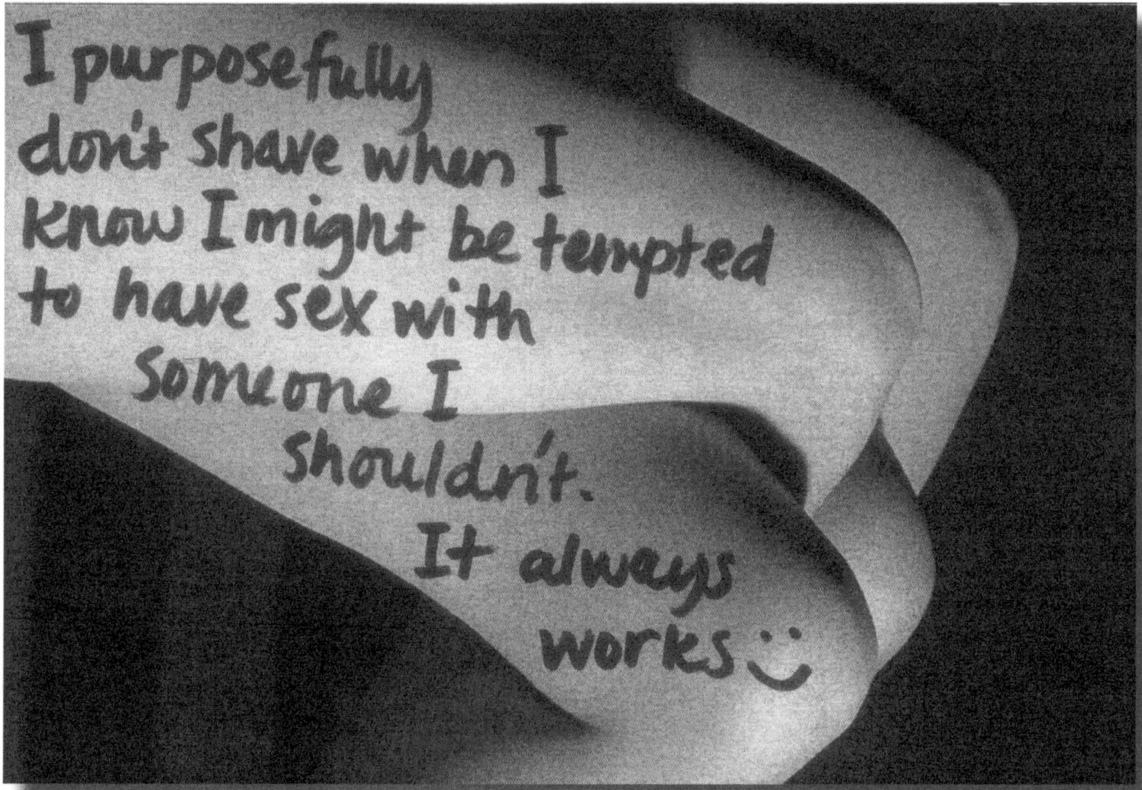
I purposefully
don't shave when I
know I might be tempted
to have sex with
someone I
shouldn't.
It always
works :)

i tried to commit suicide. they suspended me for it.

I worry that my candid SLEEP TALK will one day cost me my marriage

Crater Lake

Being a firefighter helped me find God.

As being
a
Conservadox
Jew,
I dressed up
in a
Santa Claus
outfit
to deliver
gifts to
needy
children,

I'M AN ARTIST. SOMETIMES I GIVE MY Pottery + Paintings TO GOODWILL IN HOPES That SomeONE WILL FALL IN Love With THEM.

When another woman steals your man the best revenge is to let her keep him!

SOMETIMES I AM ENVIOUS OF WOMEN UNBURDENED BY THE FREEDOM TO BE ANYTHING THEY WANT TO BE WHEN THEY GROW UP.

15162

T

University of Utah
Hospitals & Clinics

I change
all of the presets
to NPR —

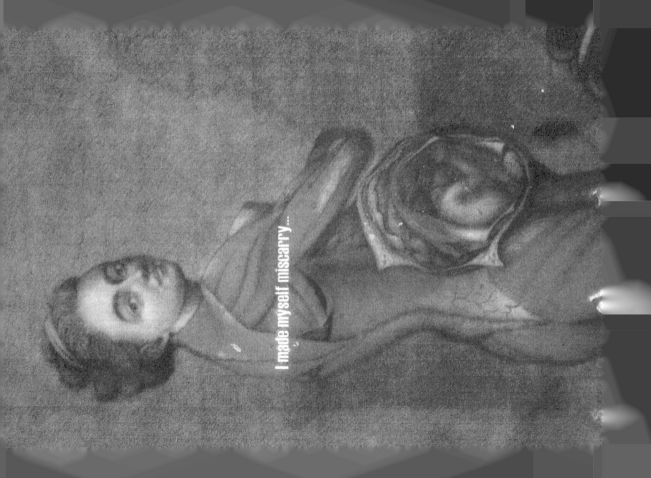

I made myself miscarry...

18

For the past **TEN WONDERFUL YEARS**
my daughter and I have shared this hobby.

But if we put **THIS ONE** in the map,
it will come to an end.

So I
am sending **HAWAI'I** to
Post Secret...

...and telling her we have to
KEEP LOOKING.

The night skyline of downtown ▮▮▮▮ dominated by the tallest building in North America at ▮▮▮ feet.

Photo © Juel Dexter/Unicorn Stock Photography

My dad is my hero. He's dedicated his life to God and his faith, and made me a better person.

So if there isn't a Heaven, I **WILL** kick some one's **ASS.**

Post Secret
13345 Copper Ridge
Rd.
Germantown, MD
20874-
3454

I believe most people don't give Jesus a fair chance to be their Friend.

I'm scared I will be killed in the line of duty...

Walking from 3014 South Ridge Drive, Chesterfield police officials prepared to brief reporters on the shooting death of Officer Ryan E. Clappelletti yesterday morning.

Chesterfield officer slain

First county policeman ever shot dead on duty

And NO ONE will tell my son how much I loved him!!!

Fatal shootout

he had only 4 months on job'

I feel bad for killing ants at the bakery I work at sometimes I tear up when I spray them.

This summer it will have been 3 years since you died.

How come I feel like I am cheating on you? You left me Remember?!

26

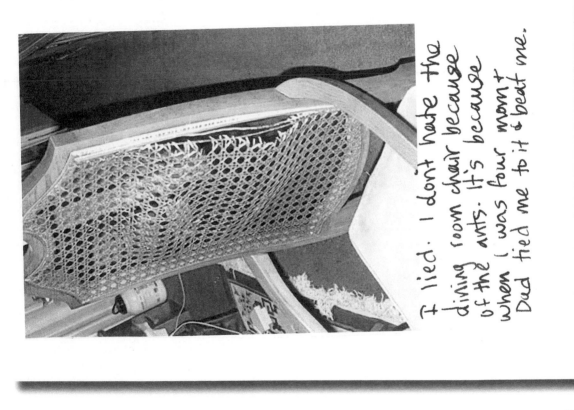

I lied. I don't hate the dining room chair because of the ants. It's because when I was four mom + Dad tied me to it & beat me.

Seeing happy families
doesn't make me sad anymore,
now that I've joined
yours.

I DIVORCED YOU

TO BE WITH SOMEONE
ELSE
EVEN THOUGH I SAID I DIDN'T

BUT NOW I WOULD GIVE
10 YEARS OF MY LIFE

TO GO BACK TO
BEING YOUR WIFE

29

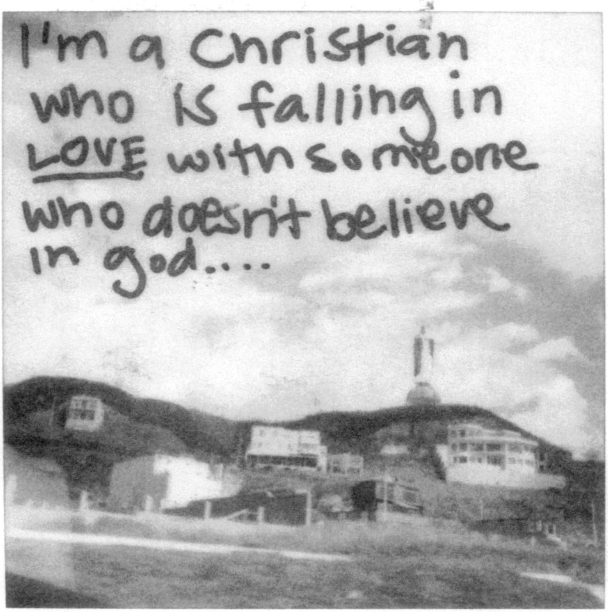

I'm a Christian
who is falling in
LOVE with someone
who doesn't believe
in god.....

I think its a beautiful
love story.

Life is more fun with my work spouse.

I woke up this
morning and
all I wanted
to do was
Call you and

ask you to
Fly across the
ocean and
be my lover.

I didnt.

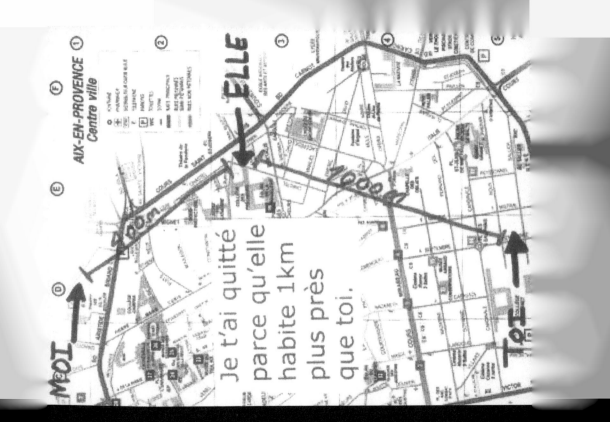

"I left you because she lives a kilometer nearer than you."

I GET THE XWORD PUZZLE EVERY WEDNES- DAY AND HOPE THERE'S A CLUE IN FRENCH SO YOU'LL CALL OR EMAIL ME FOR THE ANSWER LIKE YOU USED TO.

34

i resolve to be brave. and strong.
and proud of my life.

Happy Holidays
& New Year
Kathy the mail
carrier ☺

Lineco INC. HOLYOKE, MA 01041

Infinity™ Archival Photo Postcards

post secret
13345 copper ridge rd.
germantown, MD
20874

PostSecret
13345 Copper Ridge Rd
Germantown, MD
20874

A young man's surprising story of how he and a woman were brought together, in front of a thousand people, through a shared secret—lost, then found.

Dear Frank,

It was the day of the PostSecret event at the University of Buffalo, a day I had been looking forward to since I purchased my ticket. I had only one class that day and thought I would stop at the mall to pick up one of the books.

I went to Borders and asked the salesclerk where the PostSecret books were located. I grabbed *A Lifetime of Secrets,* began flipping through the pages, and saw a torn page. So I returned to it, and I was shocked. I had found a secret.

It was a quarter sheet of paper written on the back of a French vocabulary worksheet in red colored pencil.

I made my way to the register and bought the book. Once I got back to my car, I sent a text to my friend, who was going to the event with me later that evening, telling her I had found a secret in the book I just purchased.

When we arrived at the event, I asked my friend if it would be appropriate to share it with the audience. She encouraged me.

I made my way to the microphone, got in line and I told my story to the girl behind me and asked what she thought I should do. She was pretty emotional, crying a lot, and said, "I think you should . . . that would be great. I think the person would appreciate it."

You spoke with a few people in the balcony, and to the left of my line. Then it was my turn.

"I went to the store today to get one of your books. They didn't have the one I wanted, so I started to flip through the pages of the ones they had. And as I flipped through this one"—holding the book up for the audience—"I found a secret that someone had left in it. So I just want to share that with you tonight . . . 'I laid in your bed when everyone was downstairs and I went to your room to get a hoodie. I just wanted to see what it might have been like if I had said "yes." Since May 30, I've been in love with you.'"

While I walked back to my seat, the girl I had spoken to in line was at the microphone talking to you.

"That boy just read my secret I left in one of your books at Borders."

You could have heard a pin drop.

At the end, my friend and I got up to get in line for an autograph, and I found myself yet again face to face with the girl who had written that secret.

We got in line together and I told her my story, about how I found it and whatnot. We talked about how we were feeling at that moment. Then we exchanged names and said we would find each other and be Facebook friends. To our surprise, while we were conversing, people were taking pictures of us.

That was one of the most inspirational days of my life. I'll never forget the feeling I had when I found the secret and then met its author.

In closing, I'd like to reference one of my favorite secrets. It depicts a pregnant woman with a painting of the Earth on her belly. The text on the card read, "We're all so connected, I *desperately* wish we knew it."

BEFORE I GO ON A TRIP
I WRITE A LETTER TO MY FAMILY
JUST IN CASE I DIE.

I am afraid that we are destroying the earth, but most days I am too lazy to do much about it.

If my dog were a human, i think he'd look like brad pitt.

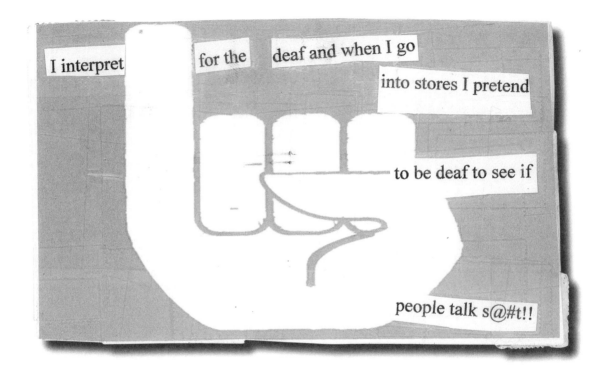

I interpret for the deaf and when I go into stores I pretend to be deaf to see if people talk s@#t!!

When I was in elementary school,
I was the fat kid.
This girl on my bus
would always make fun of me.
I remember her favorite
color was yellow.
She and the other 'popular' girls would play
clapping games and make up sayings to go with them.
When I was around (my name's Jenny)
they would sing "1-800-95-JENNY (Jenny Craig#)
she's so FAT she'll never get SKINNY."
I've lost a lot of weight
but I don't think I'll ever feel skinny.
I still hate yellow.

48

I can4 Kill myself because I'm worried the Kids with Autism I work with will wonder where I am

if i died today,

would there be anything you wish you had said to me?

I miss the wonder and excitement I used to feel for the random, everyday shit.

So tomorrow,

I'm going to Rehab!

Sometimes I text the "wrong" person...on purpose, just to start a conversation.

Love you

A stranger accidentally text messaged me the other day. I didn't delete it. I look **at it before** I go to bed at night and sometimes **during** the day. I know it wasn't meant for me...
but it's nice to pretend it was.

I cannot tell my family that I think grandpa **FAKED** his deathbed conversion to make them all feel better.

He was a lifelong **ATHEIST**, and he was one of the kindest, most decent and generous men I've ever known.

20874345446

57

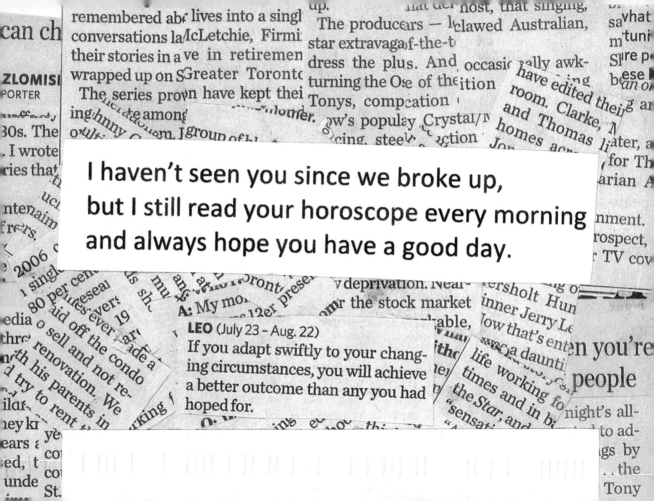

I haven't seen you since we broke up,
but I still read your horoscope every morning
and always hope you have a good day.

LEO (July 23 – Aug. 22)
If you adapt swiftly to your changing circumstances, you will achieve a better outcome than any you had hoped for.

husband of Thea. wake will be held at airchild Sons, Inc., Home, 1570 Northern rd, Manhasset, on y, May 31, from 3 to 5 9 PM, and on Wed- June 1, from 7 to 9 neral service will be the Coptic Orthodox 90 Woodbury Road, ry, NY, on Thursday, at 10 AM. In lieu of donations may be o the Prostate Cancer tion, 1250 4th Street, onica, CA. 90401.

AUT—Melvin 74, of Livingston, NJ. husband of Judy, father of Nancy d her husband Bruce and his wife Jo and his wife Go grandfather live. services will be held m-Apter-Kreitzman Funeral Chapel, on, 973-432-6600 on day, June 1. 12 noo nt Moun ry, Iselin, NJ.

— Gertrude. Of Hills, NY, beloved wife te John T. Cannon, on 2005. Tru y Wilson, was known profession- the longtime Direc- wards for the National my of Television Arts ences. She was also a Bleu trained gourmet nd cookbook author. s will take place at dy Queen of Martyrs in Forest Hills, NY, on day, June 1, at 1 pm. urvived by a daugh-

James H. Ellis fund in care of Westchester Community Foundation, 200 N. Central Park Ave, Hartsdale, NY 10530. Funeral services were held Sunday, May 29, 2005.

GOODMAN—Ruth. On May 28. Beloved wife of the late Abraham. Beloved stepmoth- er of Philip, Leonard and Morris Goodman. Beloved sister of Beth Fox of NYC, Lena Ocko a others Yetta Sternick of Tamarac, FL. Board member of the Abraham Goodman House. In lieu of flowers, contribu- tions may be made to the Kaufman Cultural Center NY, NY.

GREEN—James Wilder. The Trustees and staff of The Museum of Modern pte with sorro the pa of Wilder reen. Wild an olleague from 1956 until 1970, first working in the Department of Architec- ture & Design, as a key member of the 1964 expan- sion team and intimately running the Museum's De- part ent of Exhibitions. His fine eye and exquisite sense of style will be sorely missed. David Rockefeller Chairman Emeritus Agnes Gund President Emerita Ronald S. Lauder, Chairman Robert B. Menschel, Pres. Glenn D. Lowry, Director The Museum of Modern Art

eight grandchildren, and his sister. Born in Wloclawek, Poland on January 23, 1925. Of seven family members only he and his sister Sally survived the Holocaust. From 1939-1945 Sam survived as a prisoner in labor and exter- mination camps. He worked his way up to become Pres- ident of Valerie Sportswear. A true humanitarian, he ded- icated his life to philanthropy and helped others in need to achieve the American Dream. Shiva at 14 School House Ln. Great Neck, New York.

JOSEPH—Terr of Rye York, died on May 1 200 in Halifax, Nova Scoti mily will receive friends Wednesday, June 1, at 12 noon at the Graham Funeral Home in Rye. A memorial ervice will follow at 1 PM.

KLEIN—Victor, 65, died of cancer in the morning of May 28, 2005 at Beth Israel Hospital. Devoted husband of Dorothy and loving father of Emily, caregiving son of his mother, Sadie, age 99. Brother of noted, iconoclastic author of novels for young people, Norma Klein. Himself a hospital social worker. Also well-versed in art history and connoisseur of classical music. Loyal to friends over decades. Donations in his memory may be made to the Sierra Club.

foss and celebrate his life. Stephen J. Sweeny, Ph.D. President Michael Ambler, Esq. Chair, Board of Trustees

PERRIN—Forrest G. Pianist, musical director, and society orchestra leader, died of pneumonia on Friday, May 27th, 2005, in New York City at the age of 88. He is survived by his loving wife Lesley Da- vison Perrin; two children, Wendy Perrin Baker and Christopher Scott Perrin; two grandchildren, Charlie Baker and Douglas Baker; and sister Margaret Perrin of Atlanta. former was a partner in ABC Radio's Piano Playhouse. Everybody loved him for his kindness, good na- ture, quick wit, and wonderful talent. Contributions may be made to the charity of your choice.

SCHAAP—Walter. You were our very special friend and enriched all our lives. Delia and Bill and Family

SHAPIRO—Ruth. On May 29, at age 87. Widow of Mac Sha- piro. A longtime public school secretary, she is mourned by her children Judy and David Feigin, Steven and Nancy Shapiro, her grandchildren Matthew, Eric and Sam, and her great-granddaughter Daphne Michelle. Services at

and Sheila brother of Dearest gra ley, Sarah Gregg and and Peter stepfather Ned Norris Sam Norris Grodman, a stepfather of Bretell and Matthew N service will June 2 at 3: thew's Chur St., Bedford 914-234-9636. request. Cor gal Services Madison Av or Brooklyn Corporation MacCrate In 256-260 Broc New York 11

R—Ha Legal Serv "A" joins a ler's family in mournin Judge Tyler involvemen worthwhile longterm cl justice to successful c tional legal against tho to elimina Nixon Adm recently h pillar of sup borhood. free lego

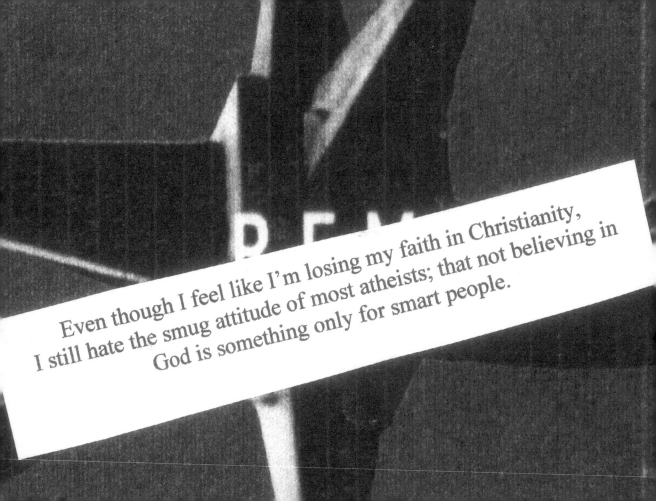

Even though I feel like I'm losing my faith in Christianity, I still hate the smug attitude of most atheists; that not believing in God is something only for smart people.

When I cook alone, I always pretend I'm cooking for The Food Network (audience and all...)

I'm afraid there will be nothing outstanding or interesting to say about me in my obituary.

3 years ago,
I sent a postcard
saying "I am 48
years old
& all I want to
be is a slut."

I am happy to
report that I
have succeeded!

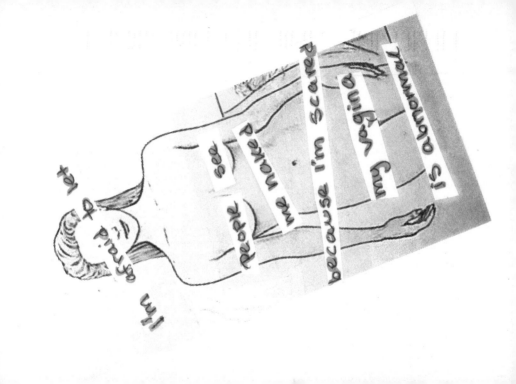

I had an entire fake conversation on my cell phone so that I could brag about my kids to the snotty neighbor who I know was listening through the fence.

67

It's not God who doesn't care, it's us.

I hope I can give my kids as great of a childhood as I had.

I'm looking forward to the challenge!

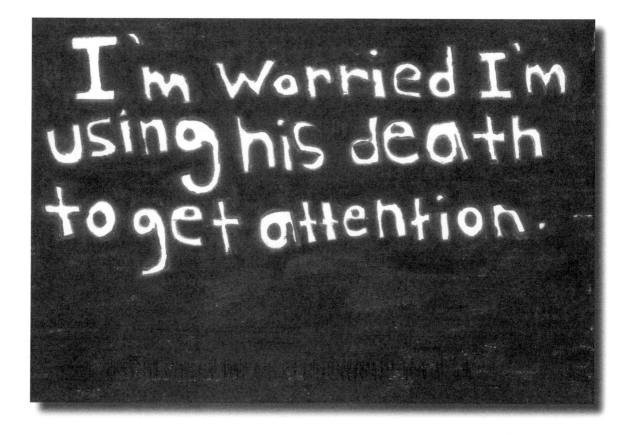

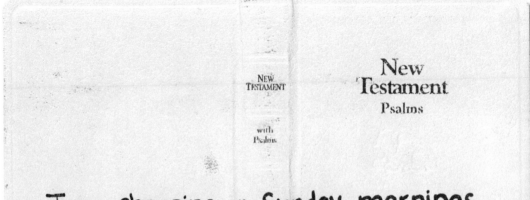

I go shopping on Sunday mornings because everyone else is at church.

72

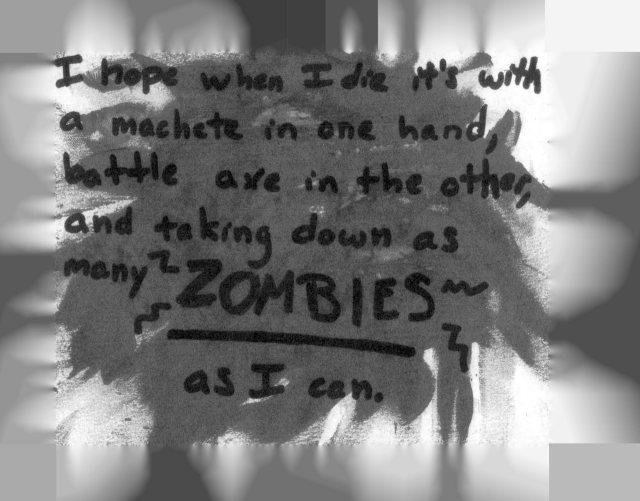

I hope when I die it's with a machete in one hand, battle axe in the other, and taking down as many ZOMBIES as I can.

I still wear your shirt.

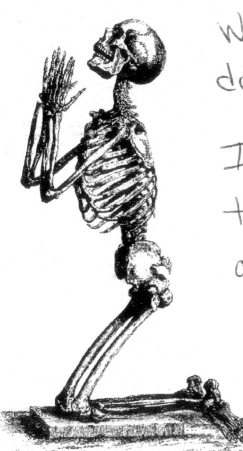

When I see people doing things I always imagine what they would look like as just a skeleton.

if ever I
was in a plane
that was going down,
rather than screaming, crying, and railing against the
inevitable, I would look out the
window, watch my death speeding
toward me, and fully appreciate
the final
experience of
my life.

I saw that
dirty Picture
on your camera

I've spent more time making this Easter basket than I have praying all year.

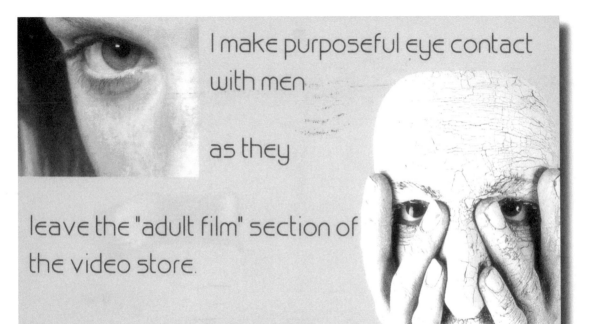

I make purposeful eye contact with men

as they

leave the "adult film" section of the video store.

I find it amusing. They don't.

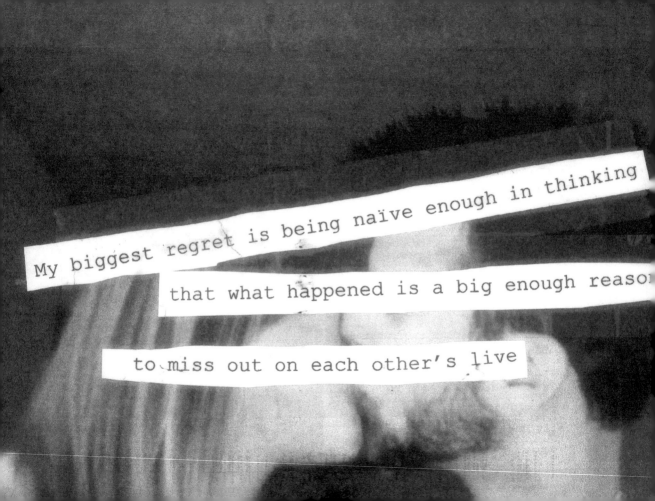

My biggest regret is being naïve enough in thinking
that what happened is a big enough reason
to miss out on each other's live

y JEFFREY GETTLEMAN

AIROBI, Kenya — The politi-
ood darkened again in Ken-
n Tuesday, with opposition
rs cooling to the idea of ne-
tions with the government
 the president unilate
e major cabinet
s, a move t
ss the co
ly.
onfires
 Vic
ted in
 the
n to
basa
e poli
claime
ably m
aising w
sident Bus
t urging "both sides
e in peaceful dialogue" and
ator Barack Obama speaking
pposition leaders by tele-
ne.

us of poor people pus
the front of a line for food r

said that evidence is widesp
that the president's party rigged

I use a

bracelet of Jesus to get

hide my cutting scars.

Kalonzo Musyoka, who came in a

talks
the o
that t
talks
cess
Union
prote
yans
rate i
 Bu
with
"a s
Kibal
mate
 "L
recog
at a
to me
nize
 Mr
Parli
tions
leade
the s
rnm
ney
 Je
State

83

As a Christian, I am supposed to love EVERYONE.

But, there's a guy at work who is

a real
JACKASS!

I judge
my co-workers
on how they
treat our
disabled
colleague.
Fraud - Prevent it!
La fraude - Prévenez-la!

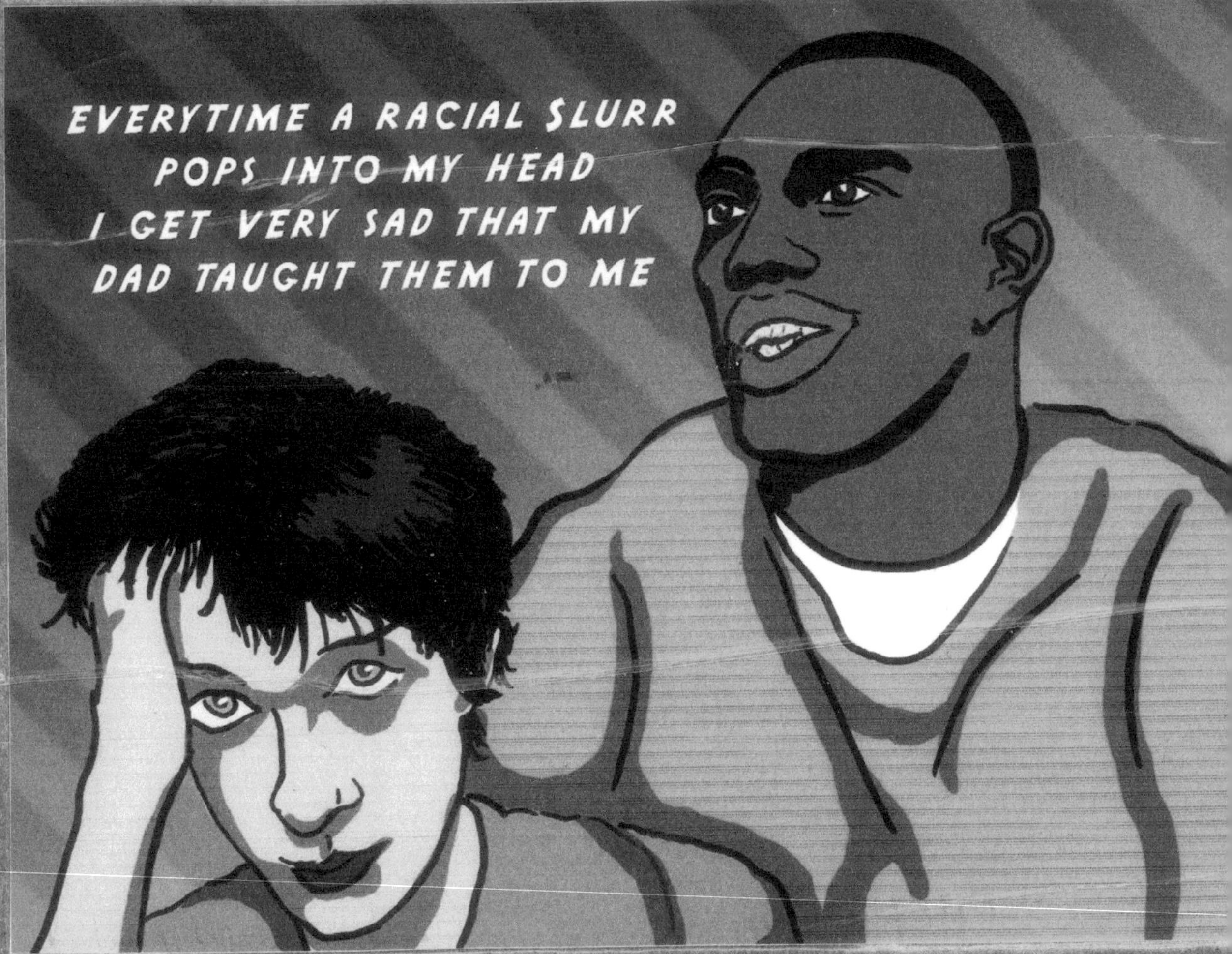

EVERYTIME A RACIAL SLURR
POPS INTO MY HEAD
I GET VERY SAD THAT MY
DAD TAUGHT THEM TO ME

When RUDE guests come to check-in

I assign them to the bad rooms

(I DO TOO)

NATURE AND WRITING are my true therapies. They make me want to live.

I know you will see this.

And I hope that you will get that feeling in the pit of your

stomach knowing that this postcard is meant for you.

I love you.

i refuse to
"hold my peace"

I WILL object.

i hope you don't invite me,
so i won't get the chance.

92

You think you are better than everyone else because you are ~Spiritual~

I should probably stop wishing on stars.

Because my wishes are coming true.

And it's really inconvienient.

I haven't taken my medication
and I know I should but it felt
so AMAZING just to cry at a movie.
The tears come and I feel
like I can do anything.

there better be sex in heaven :)

96

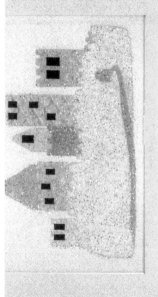

My mother was diagnosed with breast cancer last summer. Today is her Birthday. I found two Birthday cards I wanted to give her but I couldn't make up my mind, so I stuck them in a drawer until it got closer to her Birthday. I pulled them out today, and started sobbing because I couldn't make up my mind which to give to her. I kept thinking, what if this is the last Birthday card I ever give to her? Which do I choose?

I finally made a decision.

If she makes it to her next Birthday, I don't want to give her the other card I cried over, and if she doesn't, I don't want to come across it next year, so I'm sending it to Post Secret. Happy Birthday, Mom. I love you.

(front)

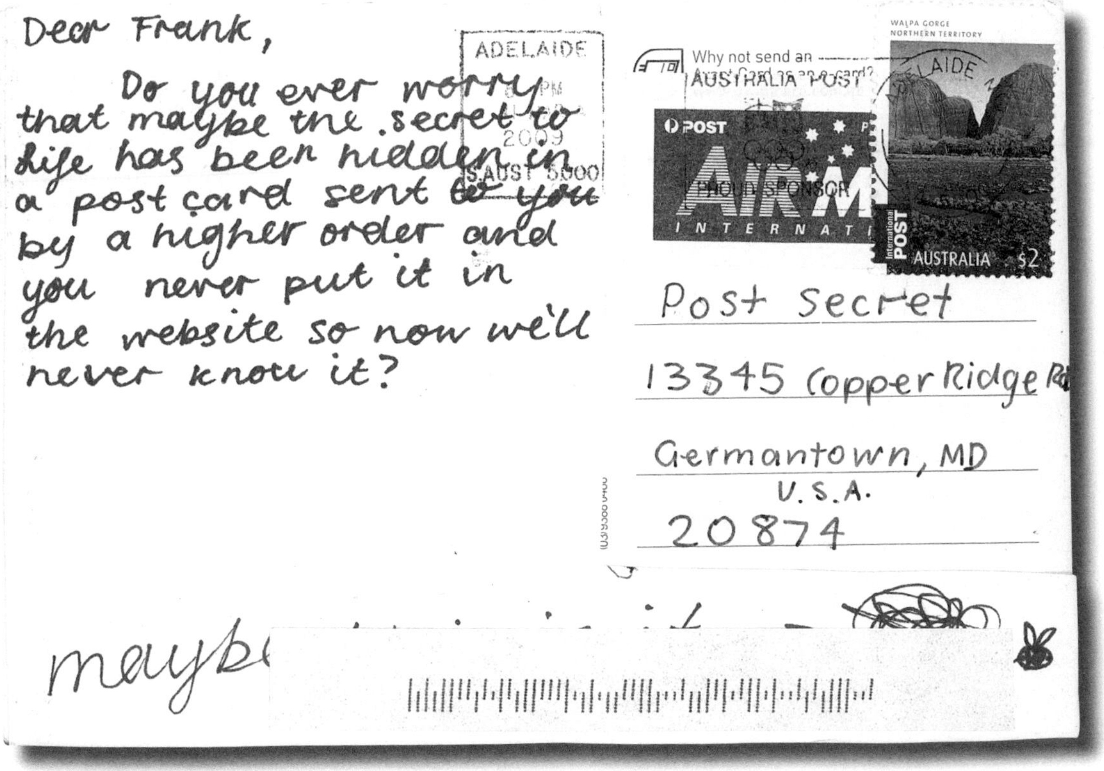

Dear Frank,

Do you ever worry that maybe the secret to life has been hidden in a post card sent ~~to you~~ by a higher order and you never put it in the website so now we'll never know it?

Post secret

13345 Copper Ridge R

Germantown, MD
U.S.A.
20874

maybe

(back)

Postsecret
13345 Copper Ridge Rd
Germantown, Md
20874

At the "All Faiths Beautiful" exhibit, visitors were invited to share their secrets. What follows is a selection from the hundreds that were collected.

I don't know what's at the end. But I think knowing would suck.

I am anything but religious but I have witnessed miracles.

I'm Jewish and well endowed. Seriously.

I was twelve. I thought I was going to live forever. My grandmother became very ill. I asked God to take my immortality in trade for my grandmother. She lived.

I don't tell anyone I'm an atheist because I'm afraid they won't let their kids play with my son.

Ever since I was a little girl I was afraid of bathrooms that had toilets with black seats on them. I'm 39—and they still freak me out.

I fell madly in love over free books at "The Book Thing" in Baltimore.

I didn't believe in God until my cancer patients made me question my assumptions.

My son laughs at boys who knot their ties improperly. He can't imagine not having a father to learn from. That will always separate us.

I went to the museum to meet chicks. I found out I was a chicken.

I wish I had a secret to share that would help all of you in the same way that you all have helped me.

I forged my dad's signature on a "Do Not Resuscitate" form.

Religious people fear hell—Spiritual people have walked thru it.

After careful consideration over the course of 61 years, I have concluded that I am an "Apathist"—I don't know and I don't care.

I'm afraid I'm not going to make it into heaven because I masturbate (a lot).

Every time I feel I'm about to lose my faith in humanity . . . a stranger does something to change my mind.

I believe service to strangers is holier than church service.

I love to sneeze! I'm old and it's the closest thing I get to an orgasm anymore.

Why's there stuff?

I thought that I had gained an interest in Buddhism on my spiritual path to help me achieve inner stillness. . . . Now I understand that I found it to lead me to you.

Before I can use a public urinal I've to spit into it, I don't know why, I just do.

I believe in a divine mystery waiting patiently for our children to discover.

My Secret is

My Goal is to become a successful writer and a artist, and to prove to people that what you want to become when you are older, be it, and don't let people tell you that is stupid, and if they do, ignore them and show them that you can be whatever you want, if you just try.

Utilisation de notre tampon en pur coton organique certifié avec applic...

1. Lavez bien vos mains avant d'insérer le tampon et après.

2. Ad...r un...pos...aquelle...vous sente...l'a...a...ez...sur la toil... accroupissez-vous ou tenez-vous debout avec un pied sur le siège de la toilette.

3. Retirez l'...licateur de l'envel...pe...u...r vous...ue le...co...et de retrait épa... sur du tube.

4. D'une main, saisissez l'applicateur entre le pouce et...aje...bi...teur...des...nar...striés...l'...dex...sur le tub... intérieur.

5. Utilisez l'autre main pour écarter délicatement la peau entourant l'orifice vaginal. Insérez le tampon en l'inclinant en...ère...et peut-...é...à la droite...sérez...pp...cateur jusqu'à ce que vos doigts touchent votre corps. Avec votre index, poussez le tube intéri...j...qu'à...e...ne...e...e vous pourrez également utiliser l'autre main pour le pousser. Le tube intérieur est maintenant dans le tube extérieur.

6. Re...z l'appli...te...u...l...ue le tampon e...lic...o...place et q...e le cor...net pend à l'extérieur de votre corps. Lorsque le tampon est correctement inséré, vous ne de...pas s...S...o...s ne vous sentez pas à l'aise...ne...us ne l'...ez pas inséré assez loin. Retirez-le et insérez-en un autre.

7. Quand changer le tampon? Selon vos besoins individuels, il se peut que vous ayez à le change...p...ouven...En tirant légèrement su... le c...et de r...rait, vous pourrez savoir si vous avez besoin de le changer. Si le tampon ne bouge pas, il n'est pas saturé et vous n'avez pas besoin de le changer. Si vous changez de tampon trop souvent, il se peut qu'il n'ait pas absorbé sa pleine capacité et que vous ne soyez pas à l'aise au moment de...e...U...ne...e po...re porté pen... de...us de r...ec...ires...

8. Lorsque vous désirez retirer le tampon, tirez délicatement sur le cordonnet de retrait dans le m...me angle que vous avez utilisé pour l'insérer. Vérifiez alors si le tampon est intact. Sinon, vous devez sans tarder consulter un

I'm 20 and I've never used a tampon. I'm too scared to ask anyone how

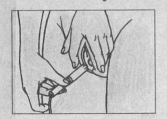
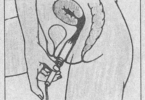
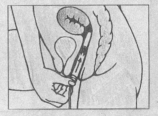

United States Naval Security Group Activity

Kamiseya, Japan

27 September 1965

1200

MEMORIAL SERVICE

ORGAN PRELUDE	Selected Music	Mr. Shimura
THE OPENING SENTENCE		Chaplain
THE INVOCATION		Chaplain
THE SELECTED SCRIPTURE READING		Chaplain
THE LAST MUSTER OF CATHOLIC SHIPMATES		Chaplain
THE PRAYER FOR THE DECEASED		Chaplain
ORGAN MEDITATION	"Ave Maria"	Mr. Shimura
THE SELECTED SCRIPTURE READING		Chaplain
THE LAST MUSTER OF PROTESTANT SHIPMATES		Chaplain
THE PRAYER FOR THE DECEASED		Chaplain
THE BENEDICTION		Chaplain
ORGAN POSTLUDE	Selected Hymns	Mr. Shimura

IN MEMORIAM

LT (JG) Ernest D. Moody, USN

SGT Paul C. Rodrigues, USMC

CT3 Gregory S. Williams, USN

L/CPL Richard H. McKown, USMC

CTSN Wayne E. Tower, USN

CTSN Dennis M. Maxweiler, USN

CTSN Wilford D. Cordell, USN

CTSN John D. House, USN

CTSN James K. Whitmun, USN

CTSN Archie R. Garofalo, USN

CTSA Roger W. Alex, USN

CTSA William F. Briley, USN

I had the key to open the door and let them out from the fire, but I forgot. They died. When I found it, I threw the key in the rice paddy on the ride back to base.

I didn't know what life was about until this.

i always feel bad when i go to church because of the kind of life i lead...

Revolution
CHURCH

Whenever I see roadkill
I close my eyes and say
a quick prayer.

Even when I'm driving.

i make stupid faces on my photo IDs so that i'll always have something in my pocket to make someone laugh

it almost always works

I could have a stepfather right now,

but I said 'no'

when my mom asked if it's okay.

PostSecret
13345 Copper Ridge Rd
Germantown, Maryland
20874-3454
USA

Suomi Finland 1 luo kla

JYVÄSKYLÄ
29.01.

When we study churches in Art History, I feel God more than I ever have before.

Rationally
I think the idea of God makes no sense
but I cannot get rid of my
Faith
No matter how hard I try

When I turned 30, I cried.

Today is another birthday.

38

I feel stronger, more alive, vivacious and more beautiful then ever before.

When my students' parents ask me if I have any children of my own, I have to remind myself not to blurt out "God no! I hate kids!"

I am a strong Christian, and I think Islam is beautiful

119

There are days when I go to church just for the chance to maybe see her smile at me.

My great-aunt died three weeks ago.

She was the last person alive who had known my late mother as a girl.

I'm terrified I will think of something I want to know about my mother, and now there's no one to ask.

I'VE JUST GOTTA SAVE MYSELF

AND THEN I'M YOURS.

123

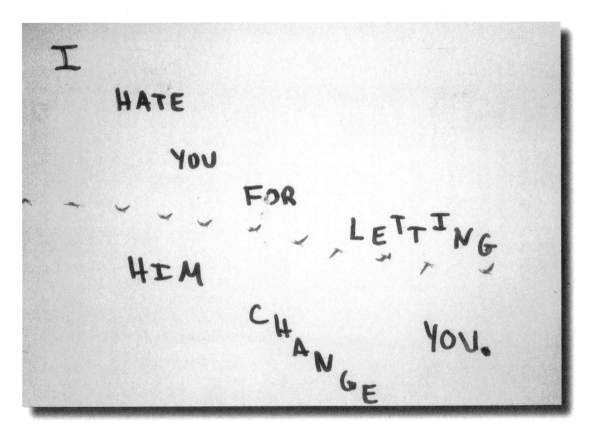

The day you broke my heart
was the day you set me free.

Thank you

1 Year
Only $14.97

Enter my subscription to *Garden&Gun* for 1 year
(6 issues) for just $14.97—a savings of 49% off
the cover price.

I know you are still with me

Because something...some faint trace of you

will stop me dead in my tracks

And I am smiling alone in the supermarket

looking at the Garden and Gun Magazine

Save 49%

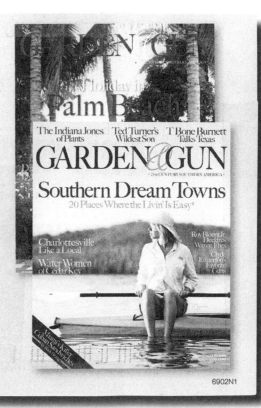

I already

knew your

secret.

Everything is going to be alright.

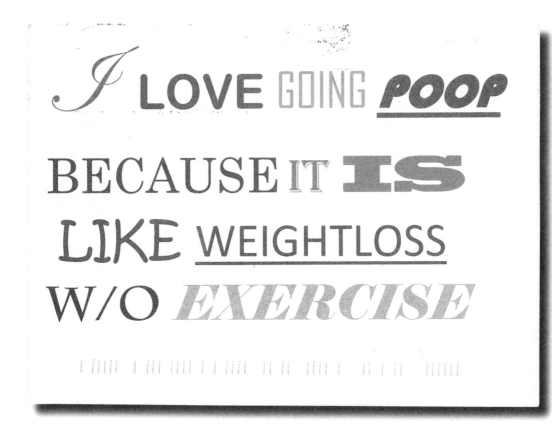

128

For 16 weeks I prayed and begged for my baby to live. God either didn't hear, couldn't be bothered, or doesn't exist. I don't care which anymore. January 4 - My baby, God, and my heart - all died.

i vowed that i would always tell whomever i have sex with about the STD you gave me.
Next to my faith and my brain, this promise is the thing that makes me feel most proud and worthwhile

when I walk my
dog, i pick up trash
on the side of the
road. yesterday, i
found $20. i felt
like GOD was saying:
thanks!

postsecret
13345 copper ridge
germantown, mD
20874

Every morning before I leave home, I clear the history on my computer. If I die during the day, I don't want family to know I look at gay porn.
No one knows.

You asked me to pray
that God would bless
your boyfriend

& I do

even though I want to marry you

I can't go to an Atlanta Falcons game

because it reminds me of my grandpa.

i came there once to try and get you back, but i when i saw you from across the street, you looked happy.

I HATE HOW THE THINGS I MISS MOST ARE THE LITTLE THINGS I NEVER NOTICED BEFORE.

139

you were the places that I wanted to go.

Now I'm all out of

DESTINATIONS

BUCURESTI - MUZEUL NATIONAL DE ISTORIE A ROMANIEI

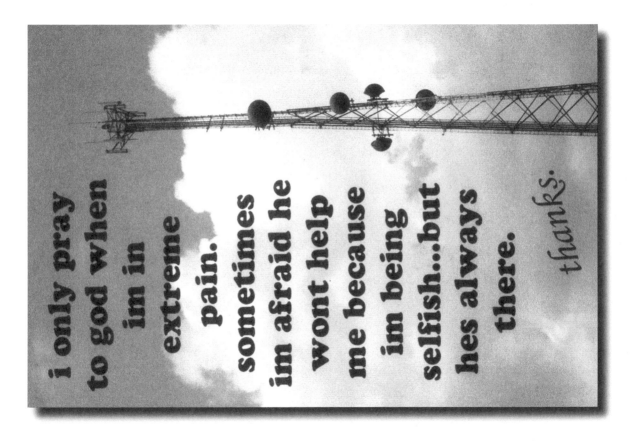

i only pray to god when im in extreme pain. sometimes im afraid he wont help me because im being selfish...but hes always there. thanks.

I am too much woman for all of the pansy ass guys at church.

(The real reason I am not married)

143

During a binge I ate all of my roommate's food…

and she's too nice to say anything.

If Jesus happens to be gay, I will still follow and love him

145

My goal in life is to have crow's feet and deep laugh lines when I'm old.

I AM AFRAID

OF GROWING UP

I'D
RATHER
THIS →
CANCER
KILL HIM
THAN
FACE
THE OVER-
WHELMING
SADONESS
THAT
OUR

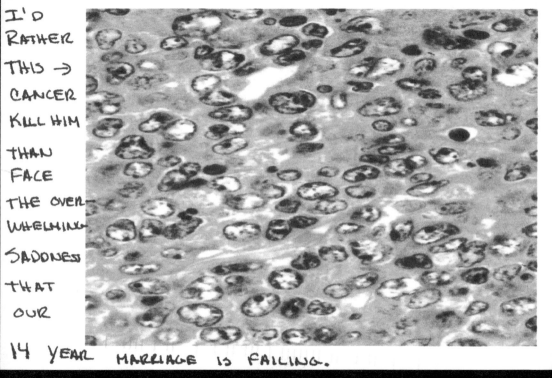

14 YEAR MARRIAGE IS FAILING.

while manic i bought a LOT
. of vintage Pottery .
now all i want to do is smash it all

CARING FOR CANCER PATIENTS HAS STOPPED MY SUICIDAL IDEATIONS

Postsecret
13345 Copper Ridge
Germantown, MD
20874

I HAVE STOPPED HOLDING IN MY FARTS WHEN I'M AROUND YOU.

To a Birthmother:

You and I have never met, though I've cried for you many times. You gave up your son so that he could have everything, and for that I love you. He has and is everything you could have ever hoped for. He'll look for you someday, and I hope he finds you. My greatest wish is that you want to be found so that you can see what a wonderful person your son has become, and all because of you and your love for him.

I love you.

PS- You're invited to our wedding!

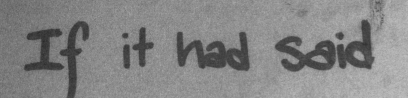

If it had said  **YES**.

I was going to **KILL** **MYSELF**

I never feared death—until I became a mom.

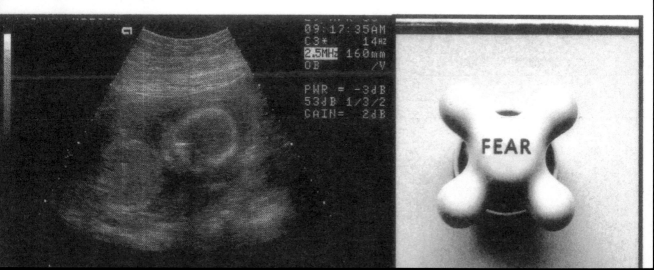

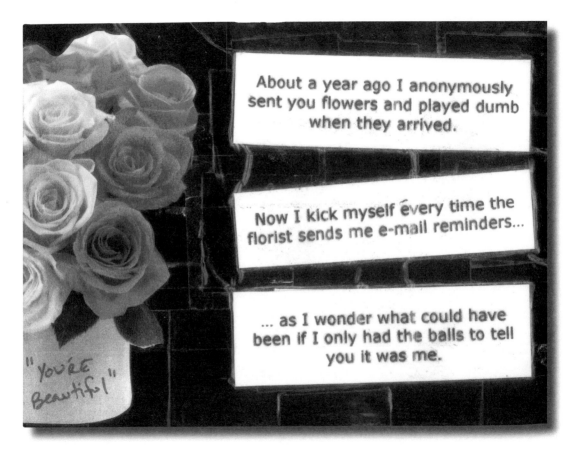

About a year ago I anonymously sent you flowers and played dumb when they arrived.

Now I kick myself every time the florist sends me e-mail reminders...

... as I wonder what could have been if I only had the balls to tell you it was me.

"YOU'RE Beautiful"

156

When two cars meet at night on a lonely country road,
when they dim their headlights for each other and

their paths cross for that short moment during their
journeys in opposite directions...

I feel like I am

NOT ALONE

in this world.

Until about three years ago, I couldn't understand what kind of a person my father had to be to cheat on my mom. I still don't understand what kind of person it takes.

I just know I'm one of them.

I look for examples everyday that prove there is more good then evil in the world. I always find them.

One day, when I was a kid, I almost *did* shoot my eye out. I aimed at a tree, the BB ricocheted, and it hit me on the left temple, very close to my left eye.

To this day, decades later, I cannot think too long on that memory because a part of me fears being transported back to that moment and walking away blind in one eye.

I've never told anyone, and not even Iraq affected me this way.

I Know I Love the man I'm with and he's the one for me...

..But sometimes I miss the thrill of searching for him.

I wanted him so badly that I slept with him, knowing he was going home to you.

Now that I know he would cheat, I don't want him anymore.

I'm sorry.

i've been slightly afraid of
toilets ever since I flooded
my aunt's house with one.

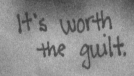

I wish you knew...
That every time you
talk about how much
you hate people who put
their children up for
Adoption... your talking
about my mom.

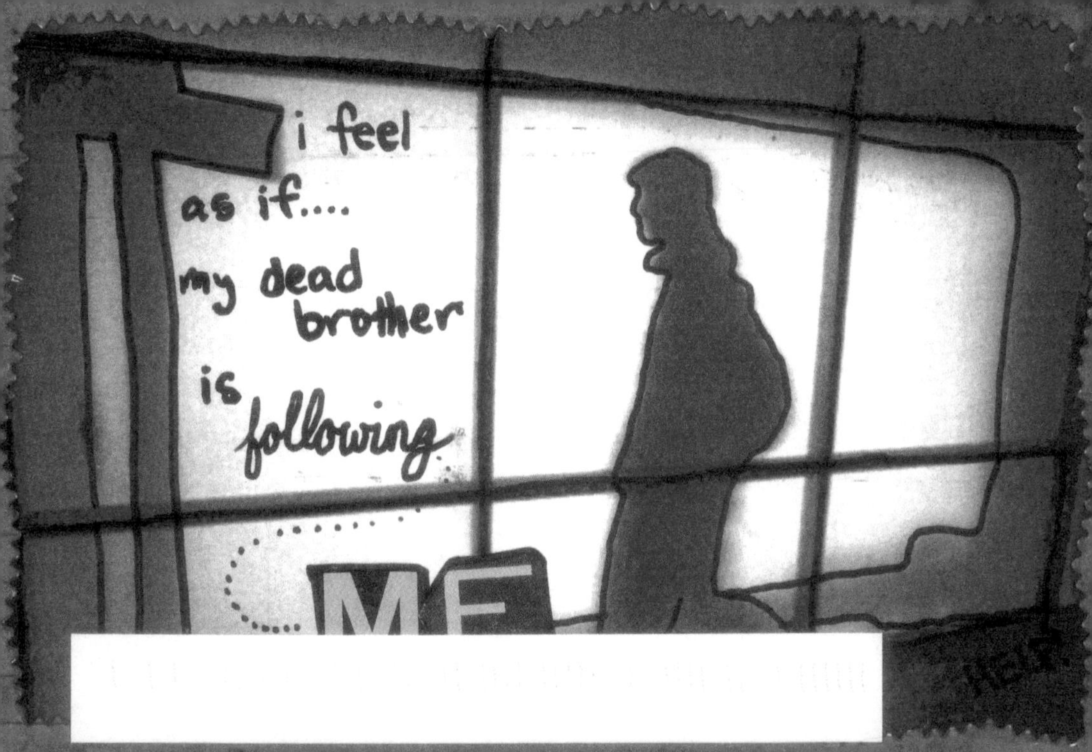

i feel
as if....
my dead brother
is following
ME

my std makes me feel slutty and dirty even
though i got it when i was in a committed
relationship

THE PROBLEM WITH MY KIND OF LONELINESS
IS THAT OTHER PEOPLE DON'T SEEM TO
CURE IT.

Sometimes I wonder if god is real, and if he is then why did he let my dad Die? And why does he talk to some people but he never talks to me, even when I talk first.

One year out of school, I asked a slender, beautiful girl to marry me. We had never even dated. But time was of the essence, and I took a chance that she would say yes. She turned me down, of course. A year later I married the woman who would become the mother of our six children. Thirty-one years later the last of our children left the nest and I retired. And when my wife inherited a fortune from her parents' estate a year later, she got her divorce. Free to travel, I roamed the country, visiting friends and relatives for a solid year. I dropped in on the slender, beautiful girl to compare notes on our lives. She still had her beautiful smile but was close to being obese. When I told her about my six children she said, "We opted not to have children. I wanted to be a dancer, you know." I drove away with the words of a poignant ballad running through my mind: "One of God's greatest gifts is unanswered prayer."

My children and ten grandchildren don't know that they owe their existence to a slender, beautiful girl who said, "No." But I know how lucky I am that she did.

Post Secret
13345 Copper Ridge Rd.
Germantown, MD
20874-3454

There is a Buddhist temple near where I live in Germantown, Maryland. I drove past it many times, until one hot August day when I stopped and went inside. I learned that every Saturday a Zen master was there to answer questions.

Later that week, I remembered a question I had carried since my early teens. I decided I would return to put it to the Zen master.

On Saturday I drove back, parked, and walked toward the small temple. About halfway there, I noticed a gazebo with a serene view of the meadow below. I was early, so I turned and walked toward the shade it offered. Resting on the weathered wood-plank floor were seven chairs, empty except for one. A large stranger with a salt-and-pepper beard offered me a friendly smile and invited me to join him. He looked like he could have been Saint Nick in the off-season.

I explained how excited I was to meet and speak with a Zen master for the first time. (I was more nervous than excited.) The stranger told me a little about his experience at the temple the week before.

"Last Saturday there was a first-timer—like you—who asked a question. The Zen master challenged him."

"Challenged him?" I repeated, while imagining what a confrontational Zen master might say to me. (Now I had even more nervous energy.)

The stranger was easy to talk with, and after a few laughs we each revealed a personal story that had brought us to the temple that day.

The story I shared was an overheard conversation between two strangers at "The Book Thing" in Baltimore a few weeks earlier:

"You seem to be searching for something. Can I help you find it?"

"I doubt it. I have been looking for the same book for about thirty years."

"Wow, what book is that?"

"I only have a feeling about it. I can't tell you an author or title or even what it's about. But as a child I have a special memory of the world it took me to."

•   •   •

They spoke a bit more, and then I heard the following exchange:

"Well, good luck finding it."

"Oh, I really don't want to find it. I have found a whole library of wonderful books during my search."

The stranger in the gazebo said the overheard conversation made him think of the sense of wonder and mystery he had felt as a child. "Before I was *trying* to find it."

The stranger then told me a story of his own. While participating in a recent seminar in Bethesda, the group leader had picked him from the audience to perform an exercise to help them all feel more comfortable. From the front of a room with hundreds of people, the leader asked him to reveal one thing about himself that no one else there would have in common.

"I was born on July 3," he said.

The group leader asked if anyone else was born on that day. A hand went up.

"I live on Old Georgetown Road," he said, trying again.

"So do I," said the instructor.

"I am writing a novel." Hands went up.

"I am taking tae kwon do." Hands went up.

"I am kind of homeless right now and living with my sister," he said. "I am living with my brother," someone voiced.

As he recounted his story, sitting in the gazebo, he told me that during that simple seminar exercise it felt as if he was having a religious experience. He said he couldn't describe it exactly, but in front of all those people he felt as if there were no strangers.

I told him about PostSecret then, and how seeing the carefully bundled secrets in my mailbox made me feel the same way.

We were late as we left the gazebo and quickly walked to the temple. I don't remember much about my conversation with the Buddhist teacher that day—I think my expectations had been too high—but I will never forget the conversation I had with the friend I made in the gazebo as I waited to ask my question.

Several months later, I saw my friend again in the audience at a Post-Secret event held at a Bethesda Barnes & Noble. I walked back to him afterward. He was getting the phone number of the woman who had been sitting next to him. We greeted each other, but he seemed preoccupied, so I left them together.

Some days as I unbundle the secrets and read each postcard, I remember my friend with the salt-and-pepper beard. I like to imagine that he married the woman I saw him with, that they adopted a large family, and that soon I will get a postcard from one of their teenage children revealing a lucid secret—that all our loneliness is just an illusion.

PostSecret
Confessions on
LIFE, DEATH
&
GOD
THE NEW POSTSECRET BOOK
www.postsecret.com
WILLIAM MORROW
An Imprint of HarperCollinsPublishers
www.harpercollins.com
I don't need this anymore
PostSecret/Frank Warren
13345 Copper Ridge Rd
Germantown, MD
20874-3454

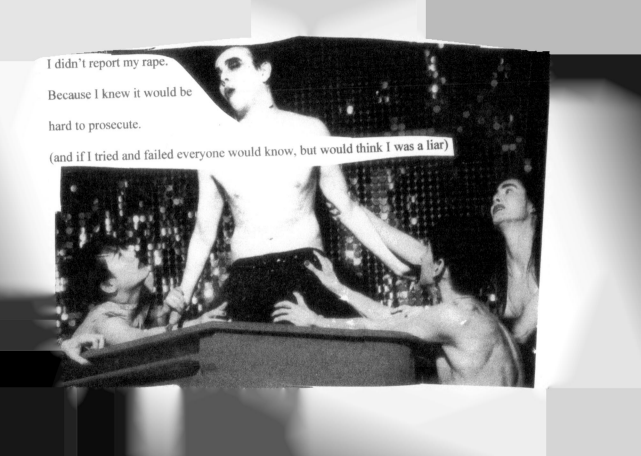

I didn't report my rape.

Because I knew it would be

hard to prosecute.

(and if I tried and failed everyone would know, but would think I was a liar)

I don't cheat on my
taxes

nor on my spouse

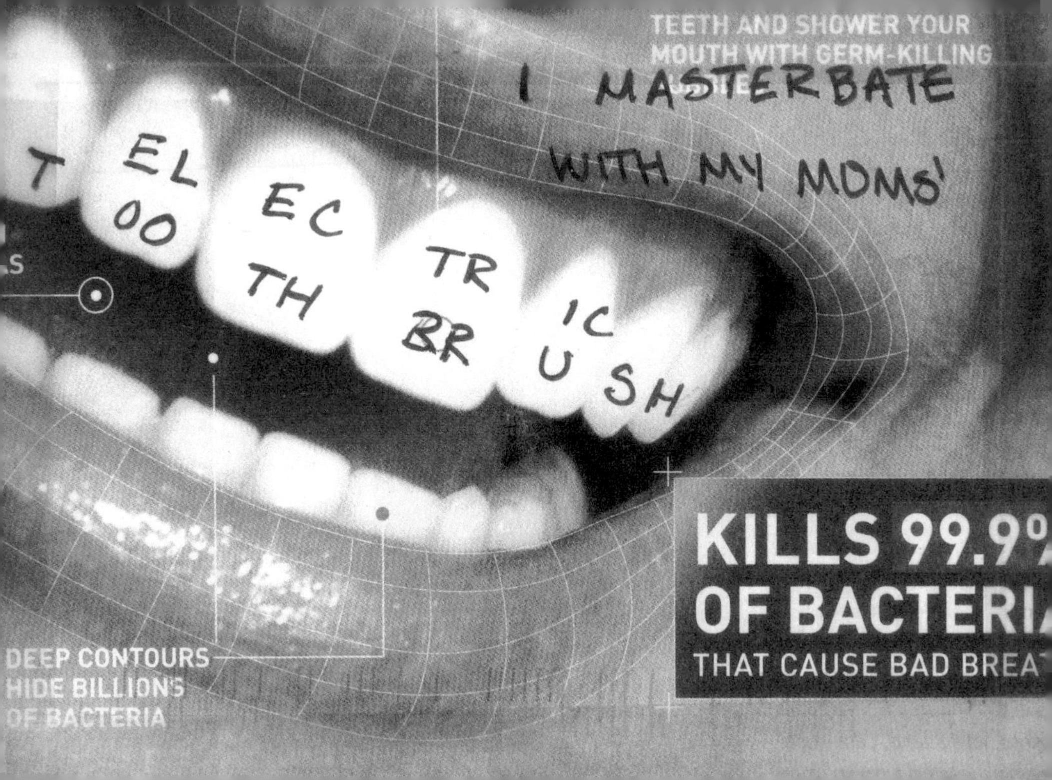
TEETH AND SHOWER YOUR
MOUTH WITH GERM-KILLING
I MASTERBATE
WITH MY MOMS'
ELECTRIC TOOTHBRUSH
DEEP CONTOURS
HIDE BILLIONS
OF BACTERIA
KILLS 99.9
OF BACTERI
THAT CAUSE BAD BREA

I met the most perfect guy for me, randomly on the beach...

...but all my life i've watched shows like csi, ncis, criminal minds and bones...and im scared to death that hes a hidden serial killer out to kill me.

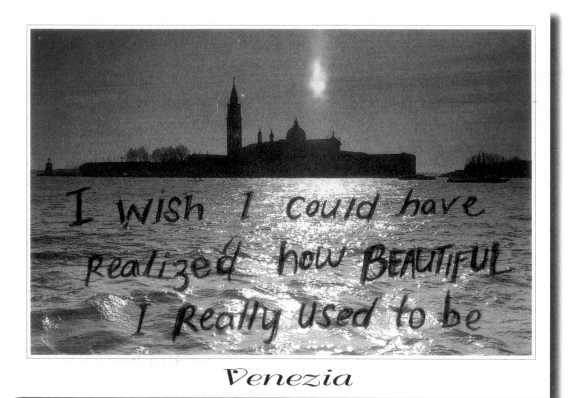

I wish I could have realized how BEAUTIFUL I Really Used to be

Venezia

Today I
realized
I am allowed
to be
HAPPY.

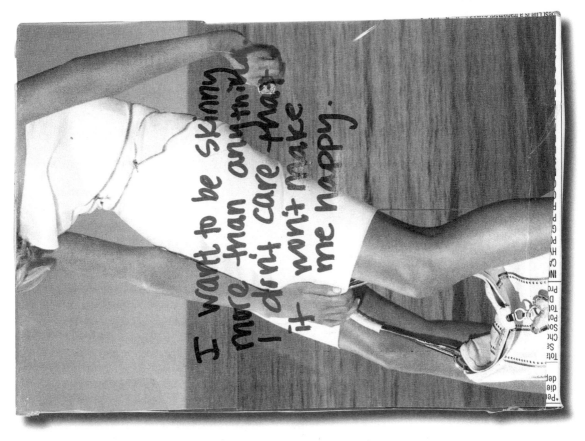

I want to be skinny more than anything. I don't care that it won't make me happy.

189

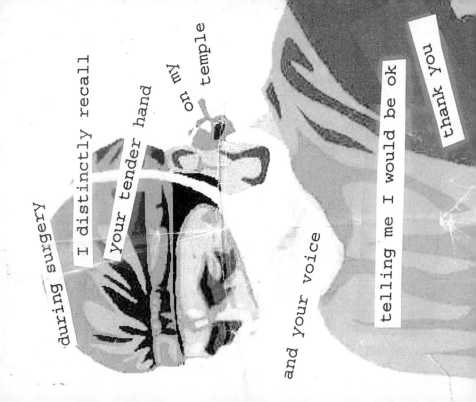

during surgery
I distinctly recall
your tender hand
on my
temple

and your voice

telling me I would be ok

thank you

Everytime I ride the subway I think about what my life would be like with each man I encounter.

When I was pregnant, I knew I would love him either way, but I was sure that our genes would produce an ugly baby.

When I look at him, it reaffirms my suspicion that karma has a payroll for both the bad and good. We cashed in, and he is BEAUTIFUL!

I'm not funny,

I just steal my jokes

from tv.

I'm worried that
if I don't stop
overanalyzing
myself and
human existence
I'm gonna
go crazy like my cousin has

I DON'T BELIEVE IN GOD BUT I'M PRETTY SURE THE DEVIL GAVE ME CANCER.

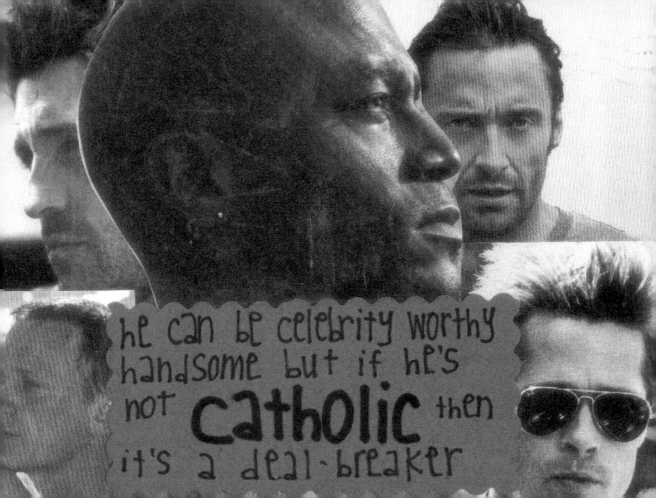

he can be celebrity worthy handsome but if he's not **catholic** then it's a deal-breaker

I'm more scared <u>to</u> believe in God than <u>not to</u>.

I CALLED IN SICK BECAUSE I COULDN'T FIND EARRINGS

THAT I WANTED

TO WEAR THAT DAY

PSALM 23:

Refrain

My heart shall sing of the day you bring. I go to the church just so I - can sing. Wipe a - way all tears, for the dawn draws near, and the world is a - bout to turn!

the young and the old, the fright-ened, the d'ring. Here, in truth,

st and the least. We come to your ing. Here, in joy,

We come to your - ing. Here, in peace

be nour-ished, healed

I want, you shep-herd you

Girl Scouts®

Being in Girl Scouts saved my childhood.

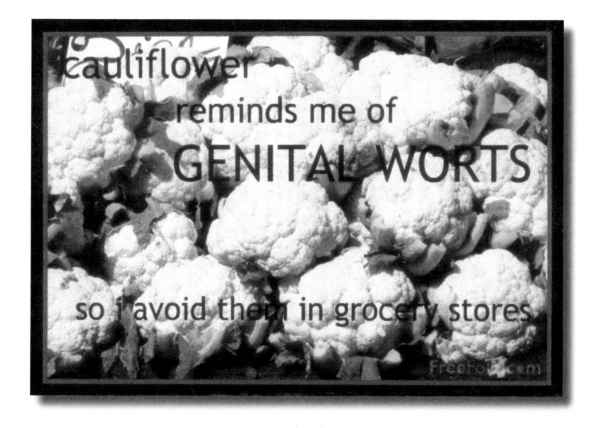

cauliflower
reminds me of
GENITAL WORTS

so i avoid them in grocery stores

When I was 14, watching you two on TV was sometimes the only thing that kept me from killing myself.

Now I'm 37 and I'm finally happy!

I wanted to say thanks. Wherever you are today, I hope you're both happy, too.

most days I
fantasize
about..

.. incurable cancer
or
the apocalypse
because only under those two
circumstances could I justify
smoking cigarettes again.

i keep meaning to tell you it wasn't cancer. She died by suicide. I'm so ashamed.

210

I tell everyone I take the stairs to be environmentally friendly, but I'm really just afraid of elevators.

I wish I had been weirder in high school.

The Trimarc Freeway Service Patrol is a free community service provided by the Kentucky Transportation Cabinet, Indiana Department of Transporation, Federal Highway Administration, and TRIMARC. The TRIMARC Vans patrol our highways to assist motorists and public safety officers. Your comments are vital to the evaluation and continuation of this program.

53

You were helped by: Toby ~~████~~

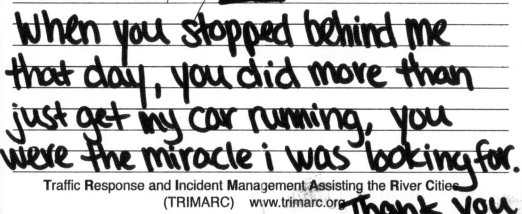

When you stopped behind me that day, you did more than just get my car running, you were the miracle i was looking for.

Traffic Response and Incident Management Assisting the River Cities (TRIMARC)   www.trimarc.org   Thank you

Only your love his death can set me free.

I used to work in a bra store

Ever since, I can't help mentally guessing strangers' bra sizes

You are invited to anonymously contribute a secret to a group art project. Your secret can be a regret, fear, betrayal, desire, confession or childhood humiliation. Reveal anything - as long as it is true and you have never shared it with anyone before.

Steps:

I stopped mailing in my secrets because I never want them to end up in one of the post secret books ever again.

SEE A SECRET
www.postsecret.com

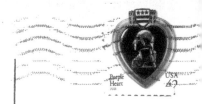

PostSecret
13345 Copper Ridge Rd
Germantown, Maryland
20874-3454

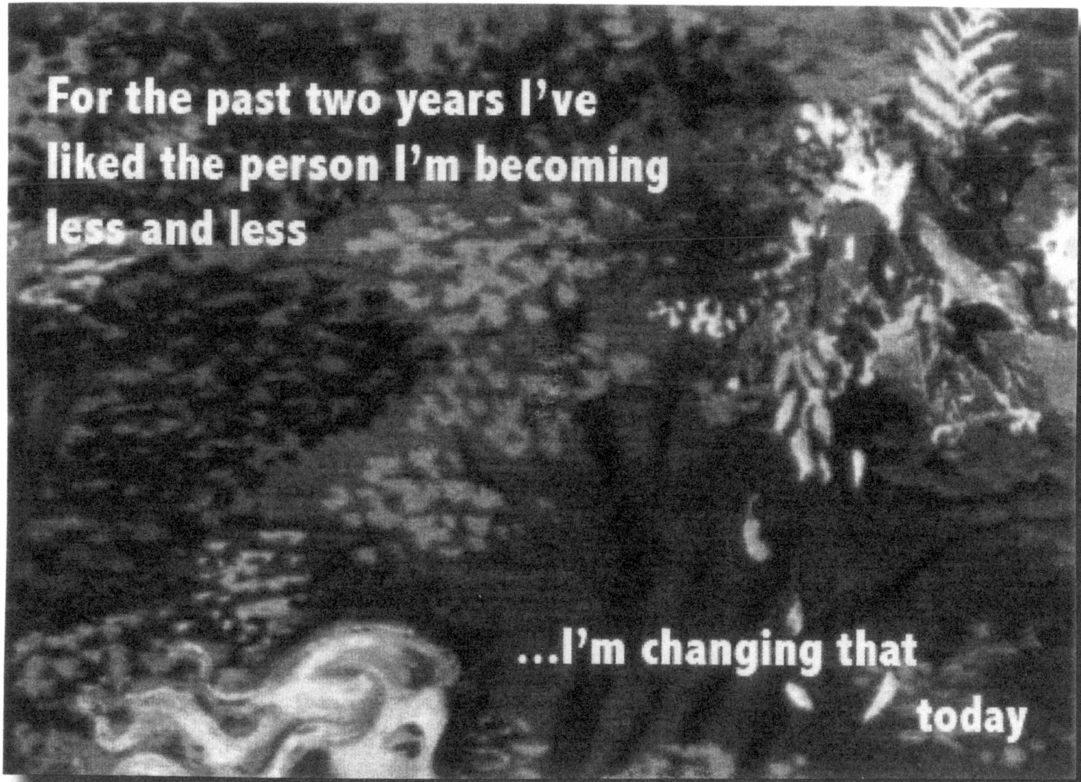

For the past two years I've liked the person I'm becoming less and less

...I'm changing that

today

I always kept my phone unlisted
so my unknown father couldn't find me

I know he wasn't looking
But I could pretend I didn't know

Just because I don't believe in religion doesn't Mean that I don't believe in

FAITH.

How do I start
this conversation?
I have no idea.
I wish I did,
mom.

Wishing You Peace

My husband and I were friends with her and her husband

My husband and I were friends with her and her husband

It only took about 4 hours after she unexpectedly died

for me to start fantasizing about her husband

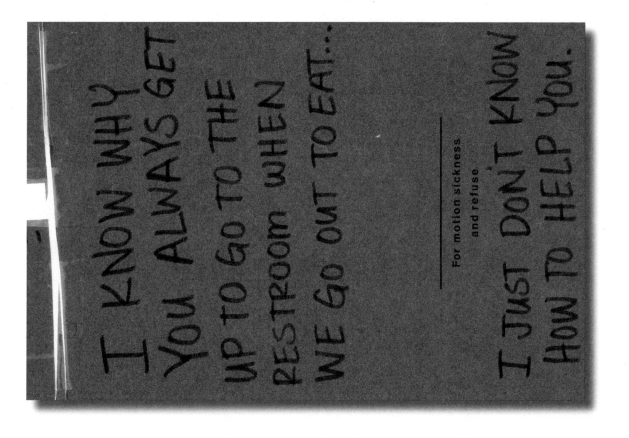

I KNOW WHY
YOU ALWAYS GET
UP TO GO TO THE
RESTROOM WHEN
WE GO OUT TO EAT...

For motion sickness
and refuse

I JUST DON'T KNOW
HOW TO HELP YOU.

226

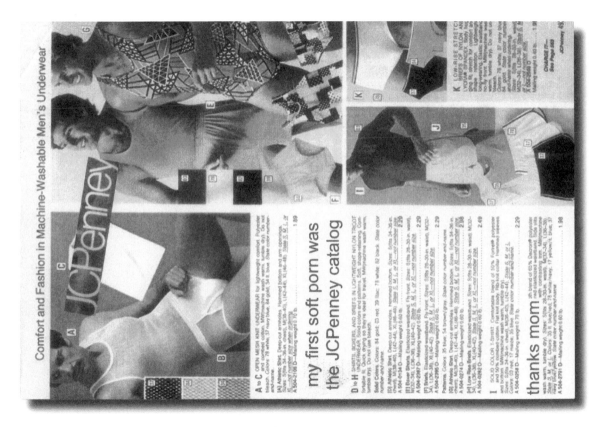

my first soft porn was
the JCPenney catalog

thanks mom

227

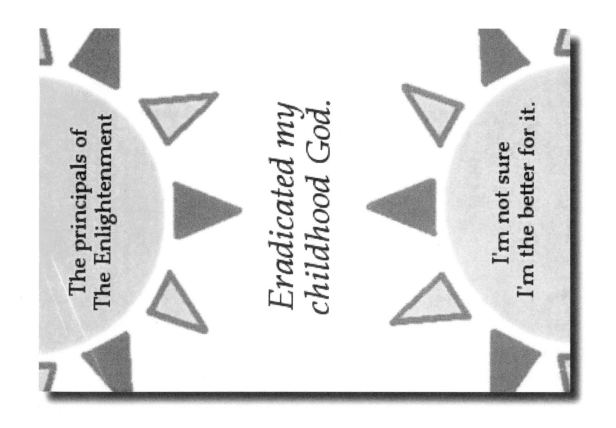

The principals of
The Enlightenment

*Eradicated my
childhood God.*

I'm not sure
I'm the better for it.

228

When I make love to my wife, I think about older women.

Every time I go to a friend's wedding I buy a new dress.

Iowa

I call them my "I'M-GLAD-I'M-NOT-MARRYING-HIM" dresses...

230

If oblivion is all there is when we die,
If nothing happens other than
Suffering ends, or
A happy life was lived, or
An evil life was snuffed out, or
A boring life is at last over,
I think that's a wonderful alternative
To Heaven and Hell,
And I'd choose oblivion.

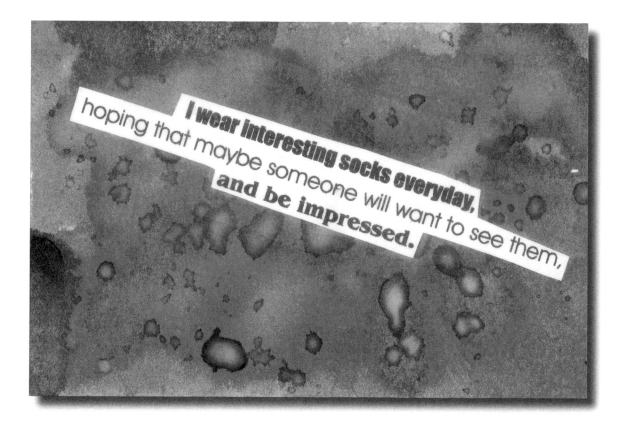

I wear interesting socks everyday, hoping that maybe someone will want to see them, and be impressed.

I judge people by the socks they wear.

Come unto me, all ye that labour and are heavy laden, and I will give you
rest.... Matt. 11:28
I Wish My Dad Would Stop Being A
Preacher and Chill With Me Instead

238

I'm always the guy with the camera..... but never in the picture.

I have fallen in love with the man who took this picture of me.

I have
to lie to
my fiance
anytime we
look through
books for ideas
about our vows

My
promises
to her have
been on
paper for
months

When I look like I'm praying I'm really daydreaming about hostage situations.

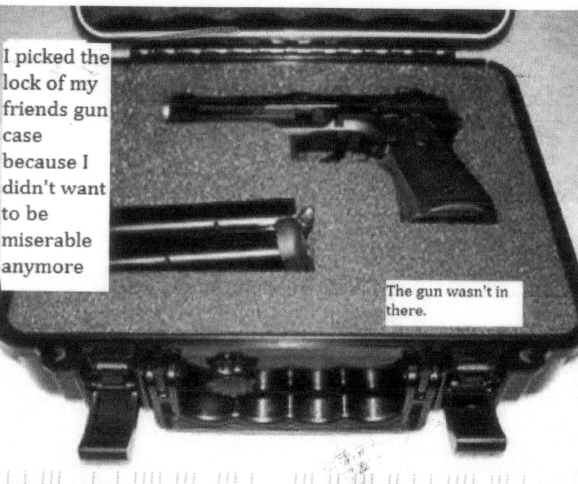

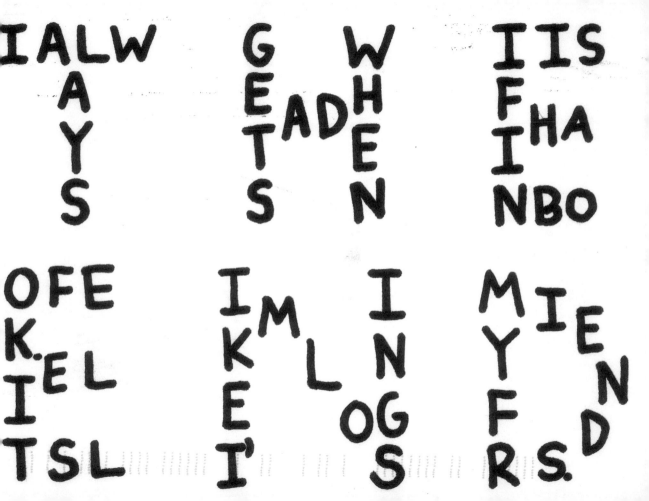

I am a **LAWYER** who spends 90% of my day **BILLING CLIENTS** while I **SURF** the Internet.

I meditate on the toilet.
(you should try it sometime)

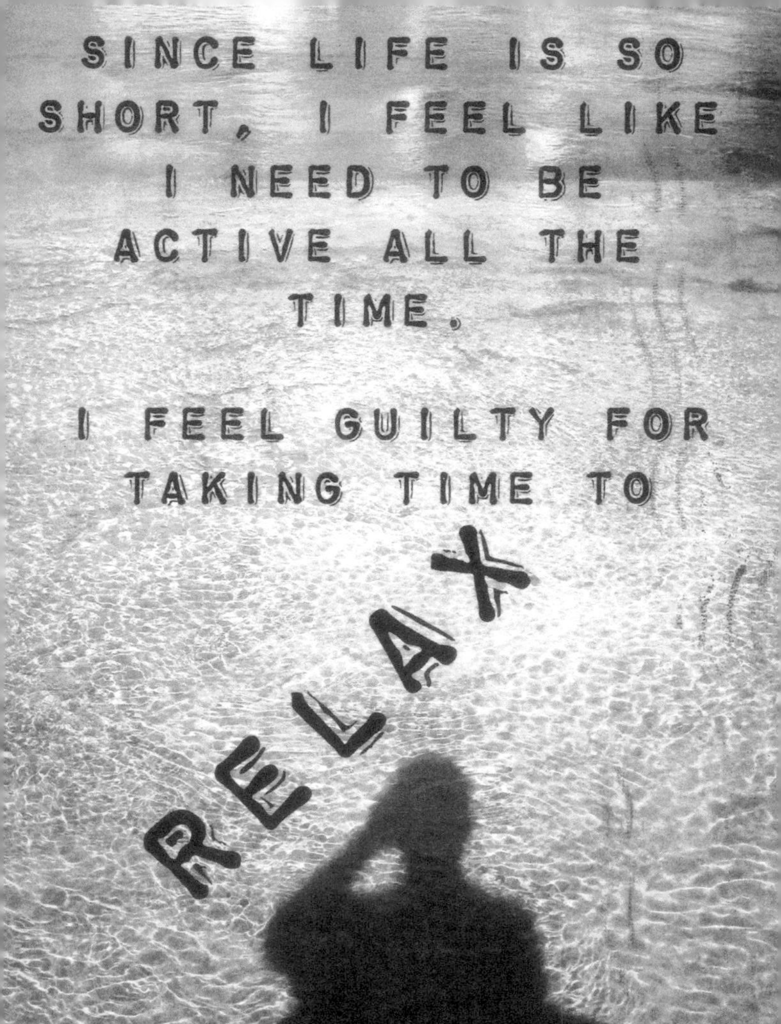

SINCE LIFE IS SO
SHORT, I FEEL LIKE
I NEED TO BE
ACTIVE ALL THE
TIME.

I FEEL GUILTY FOR
TAKING TIME TO

RELAX

I was afraid if they found out I had cheated on their father, they would never forgive me... ...turns out that the secrets they were keeping about him are a million times worse.

I'm a psychotherapist who helps people every day, but I can't help me.

I'm going to die alone; that's what REALLY upsets me.

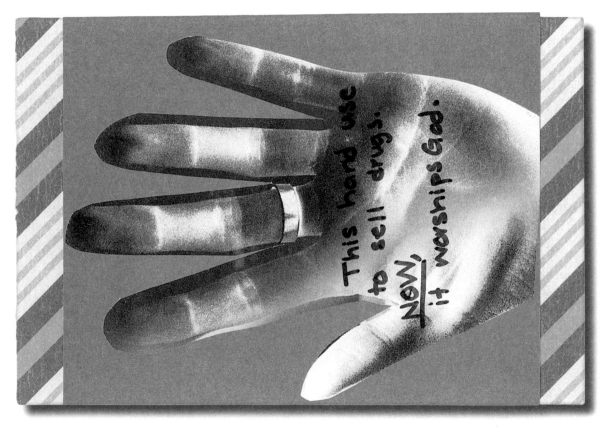

252

I LOVE YOU SO MUCH

BECAUSE OF YOUR INTENSE

FAITH IN CHRISTIANITY.

BUT SOMETIMES, I'D

LIKE TO JUST

RIP YOUR CLOTHES OFF

AND BE THE CAUSE OF

YOUR DOWNFALL.

253

I spent my childhood wishing I was an adult and now I spend my adulthood wishing I was a child.

254

i hope your wife knows what you did and that she's a stronger woman now because of it.

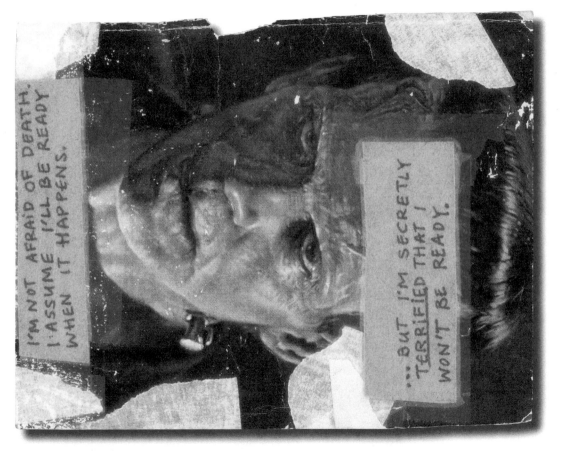

256

I caught my boyfriend peeing in the shower.
I pretended to be mad.

He doesn't know I do it too.

But I aim for his feet.

When I was a little girl, the dance teacher stopped the class, made me hold my position, and told the class to list all the things I was doing wrong.

Every girl had something to say.

I can still hear their voices

when I DANCE.

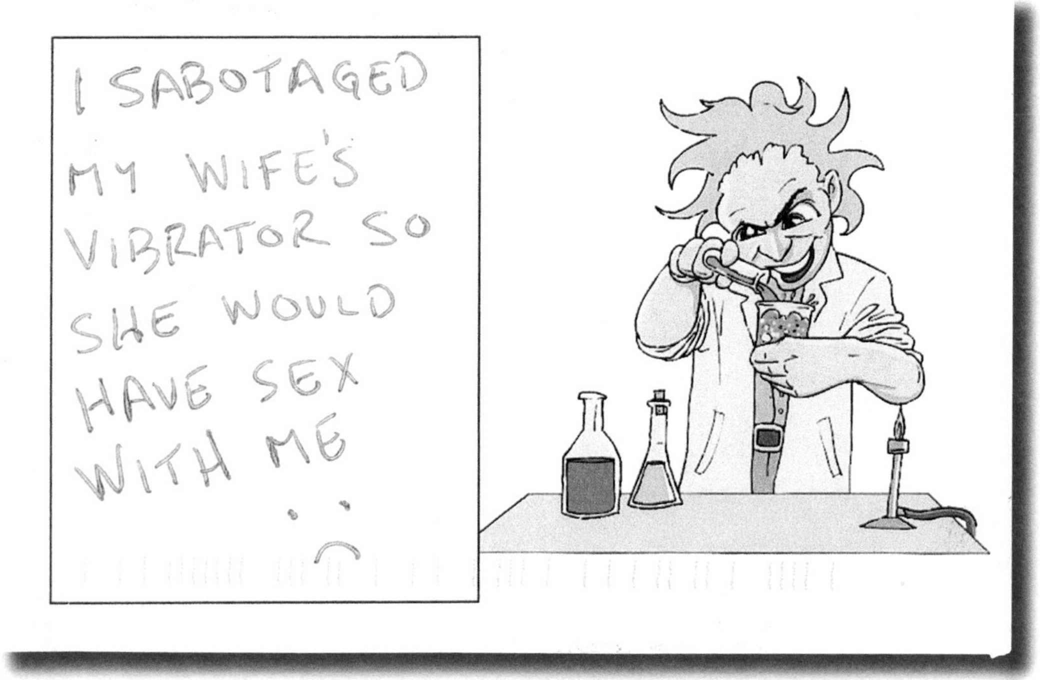
I SABOTAGED MY WIFE'S VIBRATOR SO SHE WOULD HAVE SEX WITH ME

I've never loved you more than when you crashed the car, called me ugly, gave me scars, or introduced me to heroin. No one understands.

I'm a Christian but I'm afraid to learn too much about God because I'm afraid It wont make sense and I'll stop believing.

I can't take back what you've taken away

but I can move on with what is left.

You took my childhood away from me

– but you will never have all of me ...

I

forgive

you ...

Dear God,

will you still love me if I believe in Evolution??

... My boyfriend won't.

25 YEARS AGO, I TALKED SOMEBODY OUT OF BECOMING A SUICIDE BOMBER FOR A TERRORIST ORGANIZATION.

My first roommate in college was a kleptomaniac. Her closet was FULL of clothes she had stolen from the Mall. I let people who lived on my floor steal her clothes. I

I'M just waiting for someone I can tell all my secrets to. That way, I can stop spending all my money on STAMPS.

I'm so afraid I won't remember all the people I have been.

Rebecca Hoffberger tells the story of a romantic proposal that occurred at the American Visionary Art Museum during the "All Faiths Beautiful" exhibit.

The PostSecret postcards were displayed on the wall of a circular staircase that gradually rose to the third floor of the museum. As the couple slowly went up the stairs, she read every secret. He knew she would because it had been her idea to come and see the cards.

What she did not know was that earlier he had made a special arrangement with me to replace the last postcard at the top of the stairs with a special one he had created just for her to see. When they ascended to the highest level, she read his secret:

I don't know if I believe in God, but I sure believe something great brought you into my life. If you turn around I'll ask you to marry me.

When she finished reading, she turned to see her future husband on bended knee with an illuminated jewelry box and a diamond ring. She said yes, with tears. The surprised museum patrons, who had just become witnesses, broke into spontaneous applause.

Epilogue

The postcards that were originally displayed in the "All Faiths Beautiful" exhibit now tour under the title "PostSecret: Confessions on Life, Death, and God." The wall text I wrote for that exhibit was originally displayed at the American Visionary Art Museum and has not changed.

When I was in high school, I attended a Pentecostal church five days a week. After every service, I approached the altar, raised my hands, and prayed fervently to speak in tongues like the other church members. Two years passed without success. I felt lost, a failure in God's eyes. I left the church and never talked about this experience. It became a spiritual secret.

In 2004, I started the PostSecret project and invited people to share their secrets with me. Since then I have received more than four hundred thousand postcards. Most of the cards are mailed anonymously and artistically express personal desires, hopes, fears, humor, and so much more.

Some of the secrets sent to me share private beliefs and uncommon faiths. Many of these cards appear as though they were created during an impulsive moment. Others are invested with painstaking detail and look like sacred objects, perhaps offering a kind of prayer.

Every secret is unique, like a fingerprint, but at a deeper level this community of confessions reveals how we are all connected by our surprising and soulful spiritual secrets. As a whole, the collection demonstrates the rich diversity of our inner faith.

Some of the voices speaking through these cards may offer you the chance to recognize one of your own secrets. For a moment you may feel less alone with a secret you might have been keeping from others, or from yourself.

This project has shown me that art can be like a new tongue that allows us to speak and pray in ways that might otherwise be impossible. And if we listen, we may come to understand that we are always on our spiritual journey—even when we feel most lost.

Frank Warren, sometimes called "the most trusted stranger in America," began collecting secrets for a community art project in 2004. Since then, more than 400,000 anonymous postcards from around the world have found their way to Warren's mailbox. The postcards have been featured in museum exhibitions, a popular music video, the bestselling Post-Secret books, and an award-winning website. PostSecret.com receives more than six million visitors every month and has won five Bloggies, including Weblog of the Year and Best American Blog. Warren was also awarded the National Mental Health Association's "for-WARD" for raising awareness and funds for suicide prevention. Warren lives in Germantown, Maryland, with his wife, daughter, and dog.   **www.postsecret.com**